Cookbook for Teens

Teen Cookbook: The Simple and Healthy Teen Cookbook: Easy and Delicious Recipes for Teens

the information is without contract or any type of guarantee assurance.

Table of Contents

Introduction

I want to thank you and congratulate you for downloading *Cookbook for Teens: Teen Cookbook: The Simple and Healthy Teen Cookbook: Easy and Delicious Recipes for Teenagers*! Today, you can go into any grocery store and buy frozen pizza, pre- made wings, and microwave waffles. There are thousands of food products that only take minutes to make and require very little skill and effort on your part. And while these simple, microwavable meals are delicious, they are preserved with many added sugars and salts. I'm sure you may be tired of hearing how bad preservatives for you, but the health effects of regularly consuming these products can really impact your life. The excess salt and sugar consumption will lead to excess bloating, excess production of oils on your skin, acne breakouts, dehydration, and a weakened immune system.

So what are you supposed to eat instead when you are looking for food and your parents don't have time make a meal for you? The simple answer is to make yourself food. But many teens are unfamiliar with recipes, complimentary ingredients, and how to cook food without starting a fire. With parents often working during the day and home economic classes being cut from schools, children, teens, and young adults are at a loss on how to safely and efficiently prepare and cook food. Not only does this make teens more dependent on others to feed them, but is cause major issues later in life as young adults move out into their own homes. The most an average teenager can cook is a grilled cheese or spaghetti; which makes for insufficient meals as they are left to rely on their own knowledge and skills to prepare their own dishes when dinner isn't premade for them. Of course, you may be one of those few teens that are familiar with how to work in the kitchen and make family recipes, which is great. Regardless, this book will help you develop new skills and learn new recipes.

It is crucial to consume the necessary vitamins and minerals that promote health and wellness, or else your body, mind, and even social life will suffer. I'm sure that you have already started noticing the changes that your body is going through. And while it is uncomfortable and awkward to talk about, you need to understand how these changes can affect your overall health. Your body needs a lot of energy to go through this transition, as the chemicals in your brain change and you physically grow. The food you eat must nourish your body so that it can repair old cells and generate new ones.

This book contains proven steps and strategies on how to become a true expert in the kitchen. With over seventy recipes, you will never go hungry and will be able to maintain a healthy weight and amazing health with the meals provided in this book. There are plenty of breakfast, lunch, and dinner recipes that will fill your stomach and help you be your best and most healthy self. If you do not develop your ability to cook, then you will be completely reliant on others to provide for you, never truly gaining independence. Cooking can be fun, and it is so much easier than you realize. Trying new recipes and using different ingredients lets you explore your taste buds, figure out your likes and dislikes, and really enhance your understanding of flavors and food composition.

It's time for you to become an amazing chef! Even if you just try out one new recipe a day, over time you will develop irreplaceable skills and talents that will truly help you later on in life. So, break out the spatula and frying pan, because it's time to get cooking! Enjoy!

Chapter 1:
Cooking Terminology: Knowing Your Way Around the Kitchen

<u>Al Dente</u>- Pasta that is cooked until it just becomes firm.

<u>Bake</u>- Cooking food in the oven with dry heat.

<u>Baking Powder</u>- A mixture of baking soda, an avid, and starch/ flour.

<u>Baking Soda</u>- Sodium bicarbonate, used to neutralize acids.

<u>Baste</u>- To moisten food with a flavored liquid to keep the good from drying out as it is cooking.

<u>Beat</u>- Quickly stirring a mixture to make it smooth: typically done with a whisk, fork, or mixer.

<u>Blanch</u>- To cooking for a short amount of time in boiling water to lock in the flavor and color of a food. This is done before freezing food or to easily remove the skin from some foods; such as a potato.

<u>Blend</u>- Thoroughly combining more than one ingredient together by hand, or with a whisk, spoon, blender, or mixer.

<u>Braise</u>- To cook first by browning food, then letting it simmer in a small amount of liquid, covered over low heat.

<u>Broil</u>- To cook food on a rack or spit underneath or over direct heat. This is typically done in an oven.

<u>Brown</u>- To cook food over high heat to brown the outer layer of the food.

1

Caramelize- Heating sugar over the stove until it liquefies into a syrup.

Chop- Cutting solid food into pieces that are not exact cubes.

Clarify- Separating and removing solids from a liquid to make to clear.

Core- Removing the seeds and centers of fruits and vegetables.

Cream- The butterfat part of milk.

Cube- To cut food into tiny cubes.

Cure- Preserving meats by drying them out, and salting and/ or smoking them.

Deep Dry- Cooking food by immersing it completely into hot oil or fat.

Deglaze- Loosening brown bits from a skillet by adding water or another liquid, and then placing the pan over heat to stir and scrape the bottom of the skillet.

Dice- Cutting food in small cubes, approximately 1/8- 1/4 – inches.

Dollop – A scoop of soft food, like mashed potatoes or sour cream.

Dredge- Covering/ coating food, typically with flour or bread crumbs.

Dress- Using a dressing to coat your food, like a salad. – OR—Cleaning a fish, game, or poultry in preparation for cooking it.

<u>Drizzle</u>- Pouring a liquid, such as syrup, oil, or butter back and forth over your food in a fine, thin stream.

<u>Fillet</u>- A flat cut of boneless meat – OR – Cutting the bones from the slice of meat.

<u>Flambé</u>- Drizzling liquor over your food when it is cooking, and then igniting the food before serving it, when the alcohol is warmed.

<u>Fold</u>- Combining light ingredients with a heavy mixture by using a spatula or spoon, in an over – and- under motion.

<u>Garnish</u>- Decorating a dish to make its appearance more appealing, as well as provide enhanced flavor. This is typically done with raw vegetables, parsley, and lemon slices.

<u>Glaze</u>- Coating food with a glossy mixture, like a jelly or sauce.

<u>Grate</u>- To rub food against a jagged surface to make shredded or fine bits. Typically done with cheese, using a cheese grater.

<u>Grease</u>- Rubbing the interior of a cooking dish or pan with butter, oil, or shortening so that food doesn't stick to the bottom of the dish.

<u>Grill</u>- Cooking food on a rack over or under heat, like on a barbeque.

<u>Grind</u>- Reducing food to very small particles by using a food processor or a grinder.

<u>Knead</u>- Blending dough together with your hands to create a pliable mass.

<u>Marinate</u>- Soaking meat in a flavored liquid to enhance the flavor of meat, poultry, or fish.

Mince- Using a knife to cute food into very tiny pieces.

Pan-Broil- To cook food uncovered, in a hot pan and pouring fat and grease off the pan as the grease accumulates.

Pan- Fry- Cooking food in small amounts of fat; like butter, oil, or shortening.

Parboil- Partially cooking food by boiling it in hot water.

Pickle- Preserving meats, vegetables, or fruits in brine.

Pinch- The amount that you can hold between your thumb and forefinger.

Pit- Removing the pit/ seeds from fruit.

Poach- To cook food very gently over low heat in liquid that is barely simmering.

Puree- Mashing or grinding food in a food processor or blender until the mixture is completely smooth.

Reduce- Allowing a liquid to thicken and concentrate the flavor of the liquid by boiling it.

Render- Cooking fatty meat, like bacon, over low heat to create drippings.

Roast- Cooking a large slice of meat in an oven, uncovered, with dry heat.

Sauté- Cooking food in a small amount of fat over high heat.

Sear- Browning the surface of the meat by cooking it over high heat to seal in the meat's juices.

Shred- Cutting food into thin strips with a grater, fork, or knife.

Simmer- Cooking liquid just below boiling point so that bubbles will form but do not pop on the surface.

Steam- Cooking food on a rack or in a steamer placed over boiling water in a covered dish.

Steep- Soaking a liquid under the boiling point in order to extract the essence, typically done with tea.

Stew- Cooking food in a liquid that is covered over a low heat setting.

Stir-fry- Quickly cooking small cuts of food over high heat.

Toss- Combing ingredients with a lifting motion.

Whip- Beating food with a whisk or mixer to incorporate air into the food in order to create more volume.

Whisk- Beating ingredients with a fork or whisk so that it blends and incorporates air.

Zest- The outer peel of a citrus fruit.

Chapter 2:
17 Breakfast Recipes to Start the Day Right

1. Tangy Breakfast Quesadilla

<u>Ingredients</u>

> 2 Whole-wheat Tortillas
>
> ½ Cup of Shredded Cheddar Cheese
>
> 1 Small Granny Smith Apple, sliced thin

<u>Directions</u>:

1. This recipe is super easy to make and doesn't require the use of a stove. Just start by sprinkling a layer of cheddar cheese over one of the tortillas.

2. Next, place the apple slices evenly on top of the cheese. Then, place the second tortilla on top to create a sandwich.

3. Place the quesadilla on a microwave- safe plate and out it into the microwave. Heat in the microwave for thirty seconds, until the cheese melts.

4. Slice the quesadilla into four wedges and enjoy!

2. Pizza for Breakfast

<u>Ingredients</u>

> 1 Whole-wheat English Muffin

1/3 Cup of Shredded Mozzarella Cheese

2 Slices of Tomato

1 Egg, fried

1 tsp. of Basil, chopped

Directions:

1. Start by turning on your broiler and prepare a baking sheet with aluminum foil and cooking spray.

2. Next, cut the English muffin in half and place a slice of tomato on each half. Then, sprinkle on the shredded cheese to both muffin halves.

3. Place the muffins onto the baking sheet and set the sheet underneath the broiler. Cook until the cheese melts and is browned.

4. Remove the baking sheet from the oven and top one of the halves with the fried egg. Sprinkle the basil on top of the egg, and then top with the other muffin half to create a sandwich.

3. Oatmeal Breakfast Bars

Ingredients

1 Cup of Old-fashioned Oatmeal

½ Cup of Sliced Almonds

½ Cup of Shredded Coconut

2 Tbs. of Ground Flaxseed

1 ½ Tbs. of Butter

1/3 Cup of Organic Honey

2 Tbs. of Dark Brown Sugar

½ tsp. of Vanilla Extract

1/8 of a tsp. of Salt

½ Cup of Your Favorite Dried Fruit

Directions:

1. Keep in mind that this recipe will take a bit longer to make, so you should prepare your cooking time accordingly. This is a great treat for a weekend when you aren't rushing off to school and don't have time to cook a large meal.

2. Start by preheating your oven to 3325 degrees and preparing an 8 x 12 in. baking dish with parchment paper.

3. Next, toss together the oatmeal, coconut, and almond slices on a baking sheet and place into the oven for ten minutes. Stir the mixture occasionally, until the nuts and oatmeal are golden brown.

4. Remove the sheet from the oven and transfer the contents into a large bowl. Stir the flaxseeds into the bowl with the nuts and oatmeal.

5. Now, add the remaining ingredients into a small saucepan over medium heat, and bring the mixture to a boil. Make sure that you stir the ingredients, so that they do not stick to the bottom of the pan.

6. Next, pour in the oatmeal and almond mixture into the saucepan and stir well. Add in the dried fruit and continue stirring until the ingredients are well-combined.

7. Pour the mixture into the baking dish that is lined with parchment paper. Then, wet your fingers and gently press the oatmeal mixture into the dish so that it forms to the mold.

8. Place the dish into the oven for twenty minutes, until the oatmeal has turned a golden brown. Allow the breakfast bake to cool completely before cutting it into small serving sizes. And voila! You just you're your own homemade granola bars.

4. **Simple Toaster Pastry**

Ingredients

2 Slices of Whole-wheat or Whole Grain Bread

1 Tbs. of Softened Butter

1 ½ Tbs. of Your Favorite Jam, *or* you could use a hazelnut spread instead!

Directions:

1. Why buy a box of pop-tarts when you can just make your own at home? Start by lightly buttering both slices of bread.

2. Next, spread a layer of jam onto one of the slices, over top of the butter. Make sure that you leave a ½ in. border around the edges of the bread slice, just like the crust of a pop-tart.

3. Place the second slice of bread over top of the one with the jam. Now, cut off the crust of your sandwich and then use a fork to press down on the border of your toaster pastry. This will seal the jam

into the pastry, so that it doesn't fall out and make a mess.

4. Place your pastry into the toaster oven and heat until the bread becomes golden brown. Enjoy!

5. Overnight Crockpot Oatmeal

Ingredients

3 Tbs. of Brown Sugar

¾ Cup of Barley

½ tsp. of Ground Cinnamon

¾ Cup of Old-Fashioned Oats

A Pinch of Salt

½ Cup of Cornmeal

1 Tbs. of Vanilla Extract

1 ½ Cup of Water

Directions:

1. This recipe is super simple and requires very little effort on your part. However, the measurements in this recipe will make more than one serving, so you can store the rest of the oatmeal in the refrigerator for later!

2. Simply add all of the ingredients into a small slow cooker, and stir them together. Leave the ingredients to soak overnight.

3. In the morning, put the crockpot on high heat and let the oatmeal cook until the oat grains and barley become tender and soft.

4. Serve your tasty oatmeal with fruit and nuts, enjoy!

6. Easy Breakfast Panini

<u>Ingredients</u>

2 Eggs

½ Tbs. of Butter

1 Roll, sliced in half lengthwise

2 Thin Slices of Prosciutto, or Ham

2 Slices of Swiss Cheese

½ Tbs. of Butter

<u>Directions:</u>

1. Start creating your breakfast sandwich by cracking the eggs into a small bowl and whisking them with a fork.

2. Next, melt the butter in a frying pan over medium heat over the stove. Once the butter is melted and spread, pour the eggs into the pan. Use a spatula to scramble the eggs until they have cooked all the way through.

3. Transfer the eggs onto one of the roll halves. Then simply top it off with the cheese and prosciutto. Place the second half of the roll on top.

4. Now, melt an additional tablespoon in the skillet once more, over medium heat. Place the sandwich onto the pan and cook. Use a spatula to press the panini down, and continue cooking until the cheese melts and the bread is golden brown. Remove from heat, slice your breakfast panini in half and enjoy!

7. Easy Low- Cal Banana Pancakes

Ingredients

   1 Large Banana

   2 Eggs

   ½ tsp. of Ground Cinnamon

Directions:

1. Start by mashing the banana with a fork in a small bowl. Make sure that the fruit is entirely mashed and softened.

2. Next, crack the two eggs into the same bowl, and stir/ whisk with the banana, so that the eggs are broken down and the ingredients are completely incorporated together.

3. Heat a frying pan over medium- low heat and coat the pan with cooking spray or butter. Use a spoon to pour the batter into the pan, making large enough circles to make mini pancakes. When the underside of the pancake is golden brown, flip them over so that the other side cooks as well.

4. Remove the pancakes from the pan and enjoy!

8. Tasty Berry Omelet

Ingredients

1 Egg

½ tsp. of Grapeseed or Coconut Oil

1 Tbs. of Low-fat Milk

½ Cup of Cottage Cheese

½ tsp. of Cinnamon

½ Cup of Your Favorite Berries, chopped up

Directions:

1. Start by whisking the egg in a small bowl with the milk and cinnamon.

2. Next, heat the oil in a frying pan over medium heat. Spread the liquid across the base of the pan so that it creates an even and full circle.

3. Allow the egg to cook for a few minutes, until it becomes set. You don't have to flip this omelet over.

4. Transfer the egg onto a plate and spread a layer of cheese over it. Then, add on the berries, roll it up like a wrap, and enjoy!

9. Beans on Toast

Ingredients

8 Oz. of Butter Beans, drained and rinsed

½ tbs. of Extra Virgin Olive Oil

1 Slice of Whole- Grain Bread

½ White or Yellow Onion, diced

½ Small Red Pepper, thinly sliced

¼ tsp. of Sugar

1 Clove of Garlic, sliced in half

½ Can of Chopped Tomatoes

2 tsp. of Red Wine Vinegar

<u>Directions:</u>

1. Start off this protein- filled recipe by heating the olive oil in a small frying pan. Once the oil has heated up, add the onion and pepper into the skillet. Fry the vegetables for about ten minutes, until they become soft. Stir the pan often.

2. Next, crush one half of the garlic with the bottom of a spoon or with the blade of a knife. Now add the garlic, tomatoes, vinegar, beans, and sugar to the pan. If you want to add extra flavor, season with vegetables with paprika, salt, and pepper.

3. Cook the vegetable mixture for about another ten minutes, until it has slightly thickened.

4. While the vegetables are cooking, toast the slice of whole- grain bread. Then, use the remaining garlic to rub onto the bread for added flavor.

5. Now that your vegetables are finished cooking, spoon them onto the toast and enjoy!

10.   **Quinoa and Salmon Brunch**

Ingredients

> ¼ Cup of Quinoa
>
> 1 Egg
>
> ½ Tbs. of Extra Virgin Olive Oil
>
> ¼ Avocado, chopped
>
> 1 Oz. of Smoked Salmon, sliced

Directions:

1. Prepare the quinoa according to the instructions provided on the packaging.

2. While the quinoa is cooking, heat a frying pan over medium heat and add in the olive oil. When the oil has heated up, crack the egg into the pan. Cover the pan and let the egg cook for about three minutes, so that the yolk is slightly runny.

3. Transfer the quinoa into a bowl, and top with the egg, salmon, and avocado. Enjoy!

11. **Simple Avocado on Toast**

Ingredients

> 2 Slice of Whole- Grain Bread, lightly toasted
>
> 1 Avocado, thinly sliced
>
> 1 Tbs. of Extra Virgin Olive Oil

Directions:

1. All you have to do for this recipe is just assemble the ingredients together. Start by mashing the avocado slices with a fork. Then, add it onto your toast. Drizzle on the olive oil, and enjoy!

2. If you are feeling a little fancy and want some extra flavor, drizzle a teaspoon of lemon juice onto the avocado. Then top it off with a pinch of salt and pepper.

12. Classic Yogurt Parfait

<u>Ingredients</u>

¾ Cup of Low- Fat Greek Vanilla Yogurt

2 Tbs. of Peanut Butter

¼ Cup of Blueberries

3 Strawberries, cut into quarters

2 Tbs. of Chopped Nuts

<u>Directions:</u>

1. In a small bowl, whisk the yogurt and peanut butter until the ingredients are well combined.

2. Next, all you have to do is layer the ingredients in a tall cup. Start with a base layer of berries, then add in the yogurt, topped with the nuts and more fruit. Continue making alternating layers with the ingredients, then enjoy!

13. Five- Minute Smoothie Bowl

<u>Ingredients</u>

> 1 Cup of Frozen Raspberries or Strawberries
>
> 1 Banana
>
> ¼ Cup of Low- Fat Greek Yogurt
>
> ¼ Cup of Soy Milk
>
> ¼ Cup of Granola

<u>Directions:</u>

1. This recipe is super easy, and will only take you five minutes to make! Simply add the yogurt, fruit, and milk into a blender and pulse until smooth.

2. Pour your smoothie into a bowl and top it off with a serving of granola. You can add any extra ingredients that you like; such as nuts, peanut butter, etc.

14. Classic Egg Sandwich To Go

<u>Ingredients</u>

> 1 Egg
>
> 1 English Muffin, sliced in half and toasted
>
> 1 Slice of Cheddar Cheese
>
> 1 Slice of Tomato
>
> 2 Slices of Cooked Bacon

Directions:

1. Start by cracking your egg into a small bowl, and whisking it with some herbs, salt, and pepper for added flavor.

2. Next, pour the egg into a mug or ramekin and microwave the egg on high for about forty seconds, until it is cooked all the way through.

3. Now all you have to do is assemble your sandwich. Place the egg onto one English muffin half, followed by the cheese and tomato. Top with the other half of the muffin and enjoy!

15. Egg and Mushroom Scramble

Ingredients

2 Eggs

1 Tbs. of Extra Virgin Olive Oil

¼ of an Onion, sliced

2 Oz. of White Mushrooms

1 Cup of Baby Spinach

2 Slices of Swiss Cheese

2 tsp. of Water

Directions:

1. In a medium- size mixing bowl, whisk together the eggs and water.

2. Next, heat half a tablespoon of the olive oil in a small frying pan over medium heat. Add the onion into the pan and cover. Cook the onion for about six minutes, until it becomes tender. Stir occasionally.

3. Increase the heat of the skillet to medium- high and add in the mushrooms. Stir the mushrooms with the onions and cook for another five minutes.

4. As the mushrooms are cooking, heat another small frying pan over medium heat and add in another half a tablespoon of olive oil.

5. Add the eggs into the second frying pan and stir with a spatula to scramble them. It should take about two minutes for them to cook all the way through.

6. Add in the spinach to the eggs and fold the mixture together. Continue cooking the eggs until the spinach wilts. Then, fold in the mushroom mixture into the eggs, along with the Swiss cheese.

7. Remove your egg and mushroom scramble from the pan onto a plate and enjoy!

16. Egg Muffins

Ingredients

     3 Large Eggs

     4 Slices of Bacon, cooked

     ¼ of a Tomato, diced

     1/3 Cup of Mushrooms

1/3 Cup of Baby Spinach

Directions:

1. Preheat your oven to 375 degrees and prepare a muffin tin with cooking spray or liners.

2. Whisk the eggs in a small bowl and then stir in the rest of the ingredients.

3. Carefully divide the egg mixture among two or three muffin molds and then place the muffin sheet into the oven. Allow the eggs to cook for about twenty minutes, or until the eggs completely set.

4. Remove the muffin sheet from the oven and allow the egg muffins to cool slightly before serving.

17. Toasted Sweet Potatoes

Ingredients

1 Sweet Potato, washed and sliced in half lengthwise

½ Tbs. of Extra Virgin Olive Oil

1 tsp. of Maple Syrup

½ Cup of Low- Fat Greek Vanilla Yogurt

½ Banana, peeled and sliced

¼ Cup of Granola

Directions:

1. Preheat your oven to 400 degrees and prepare a baking sheet with aluminum foil.

2. Now, rub the olive oil all of the sweet potato halves, so that they are lightly coated. Place them down onto the baking sheet, with the cut side facing down. Place the potatoes into the oven and bake for twenty- five minutes.

3. Remove the baking sheet from the oven and carefully flip the potatoes over, so that the cut side is facing up. Then, evenly drizzle the syrup over both halves and season with a pinch of cinnamon and cardamom.

4. Place the baking sheet back into the oven for another five minutes so that the sweeteners are glazed onto the potatoes. Then, remove the sheet from the oven once again.

5. Top off your potato halves with the yogurt, banana slices, and granola. Enjoy!

Chapter 3:
15 Lunches to Last You 'Til Dinner

1. Black Bean Salad

<u>Ingredients</u>

> 8 Oz. of Black Beans, drained and rinsed
>
> ½ Tomato, diced
>
> ½ of an Avocado, chopped
>
> 2 Tbs. of Feta Cheese, crumbled

<u>For the Dressing:</u>

> 2 Tbs. of Coriander
>
> 2 Tbs. of Parsley
>
> 1 Tbs. of Sherry Vinegar
>
> 2 Tbs. of Extra Virgin Olive Oil
>
> ½ a Clove of Garlic, chopped
>
> 1 Pinch of Chili Powder
>
> 1 Pinch of Cumin

<u>Directions:</u>

1. For the dressing, simply combine all of the ingredients in a blender and set aside for later.

2. With the remaining salad ingredients, toss all of them together in a medium bowl so that the salad is evenly combined.

3. Simply drizzle the dressing onto the salad and enjoy! If there is any leftover salad, just store the rest in a container and refrigerate.

2. Vietnamese Chicken Sandwich

Ingredients

1 Boneless, Skinless Chicken Breast

1 tsp. of Extra Virgin Olive Oil

1 tsp. of Rice Vinegar

1 tsp. of Caster Sugar

1 Lime Wedge

½ Small Carrot, grated

1 Spring Onion, sliced

½ Red chili, thinly sliced

5 Baby Spinach Leaves

1 Tbs. of Chili Sauce

1 Sandwich Baguette

Directions:

1. Place the chicken breast between two piece of cling wrap, and use a rolling pin to beat it into a thinner slice of meat.

2. Heat a skillet to medium high heat and lightly coat your chicken with the olive oil. Place the chicken onto the frying pan and cook for three minutes on each side. When the chicken is cooked all the way through, transfer it onto a plate to cool for later.

3. Now, in a small bowl, stir together the sugar and rice vinegar. Then, squeeze the lime wedge into the dressing. Mix together the ingredients until the sugar completely dissolves.

4. Add the spring onion, red chili, carrot, and cucumber into the dressing and stir together.

5. Now, use a knife to split the baguette along the top of the roll. Then, place the spinach leaves on top of the bottom half of the sandwich. Shred the chicken with a fork, and then add it on top of the spinach.

6. Add the carrot and vinegar mixture onto the baguette, topped with the chili sauce. Enjoy!

3. Pizza Pasta Salad

<u>Ingredients</u>

1 Serving of Pasta

1 tsp. of Extra Virgin Olive Oil

1 Tbs. of Sundried Tomato Pesto

½ of a Large Tomato, diced

3 Tbs. of Mozzarella Cheese

3 Black Olives, sliced in half

3 Slices of Salami, sliced into thin strips

<u>Directions</u>

1. Cook the pasta in accordance with the instructions provided on the packaging. When the pasta is finished cooking, drain and rinse the noodles under cold water.

2. Next, toss the pasta with the olive oil and tomato pesto in a medium- size bowl. Now, all you have to do is simply toss in the remaining ingredients and enjoy! You can refrigerate your pizza pasta salad for up to three days.

4. **Savory Saucy Chicken**

<u>Ingredients</u>

½ Tbs. of Onion Powder

½ Tbs. of Garlic Powder

2 Tbs. of Molasses

6 Tbs. of Ketchup

1 Tbs. of Brown Sugar

1 Tbs. of Honey Mustard

1 ½ Tbs. of Apple Cider Vinegar

1 Tbs. of Ground Black Pepper

½ lb. of Boneless, Skinless Chicken Breasts, diced into ½ in. cubes

<u>Directions</u>

1. This recipe is so easy, even a preteen could make it! Start by putting all of the ingredients, except for the chicken, in a pot. Stir all of your ingredients together to make your savory sauce.

2. This is when your master chef skills come into play. The sauce should be made to your liking; so take a small taste and make sure that you like it. If not, you can add more spices, sauces, and herbs until it tastes right to you!

3. Now, turn your stove on to low heat and allow the sauce to cook for thirty minutes, stirring the contents of the pot frequently.

4. While your sauce is cooking, begin preparing your chicken. Preheat your oven to 400 degrees and prepare a baking sheet with aluminum foil and cooking spray. Place the chicken onto the sheet and put into the oven. Cook the chicken for approximately twenty- five minutes, or until the juices run clear.

5. Once the chicken ins finished cooking, remove it from the oven and transfer the cubes into a medium- size bowl. Drizzle the sauce on top of your chicken and toss so that the chicken is evenly coated. Enjoy!

5. Spicy Chicken Tacos

<u>Ingredients</u>

2 8-in. Whole- Wheat Tortillas

½ Yellow Onion, roughly chopped

½ lb. of Cooked Chicken, shredded with a fork

1 Cup of Frozen Sweet Corn

½ Red Bell Pepper, chopped

1/3 Cup of Shredded Pepper Jack Cheese

1 ½ Tbs. of Extra Virgin Olive Oil

Directions:

1. Heat the oil in a medium- size frying pan on medium- high heat. Add the chopped onion and red pepper to the skillet and cook until the pepper becomes tender.

2. While the vegetables are frying in the skillet, cook the corn according to the packaging instructions.

3. Remove the onion and pepper from the frying pan and carefully place one of the tortillas into the pan with a little drizzle of olive oil. Wait twenty seconds before adding on half of the cheese and half of the cooked vegetables.

4. Remove the tortilla from the skillet onto a plate and add the chicken on top. Repeat the process with the second tortilla, and enjoy your tacos with a side of sour cream or guacamole!

6. Cheesy Veggie Roll- Ups

Ingredients

½ Tbs. of Extra Virgin Olive Oil

½ Red Onion, diced

1 Carrot, grated

27

1 Beetroot, grated

¼ Cup of Shredded Cheddar Cheese

½ Tbs. of Thyme Leaves

1 Tbs. of Flaked Almonds

2 Tbs. of One Beaten Egg

10 Oz. Sheet of Puff Pastry

Directions:

1. Start by heating the olive oil in a skillet. When the oil has heated up, add the onion into the skillet and fry for approximately five minutes: stirring occasionally. Also, preheat your oven to 390 degrees and prepare a baking sheet with aluminum foil and cooking spray.

2. Next, add the grated carrot and beetroot into the frying pan and cook for another seven to ten minutes. Stir the vegetables until they soften. When the veggies are done cooking, transfer them into a medium- size mixing bowl.

3. Now, stir the cheese and thyme into the veggie mixture while it is still hot. Then, stir in the almonds. Chill the veggie mixture for approximately thirty minutes.

4. Unroll the puff pastry sheet and cut it into half lengthwise. Use a spoon to evenly place the vegetable filling onto the middle of both pastry halves. Brush the edges of the puff pastry with the beaten egg, and fold the sides of the pastry over, so that it covers the filling.

5. Next, turn the rolls over, putting the seams of the pastries on the underside. Place the rolls onto the baking sheet and transfer into the oven. Cook the cheesy vegetable roll ups in the oven for twenty minutes, until the crust becomes golden brown. Remove from the oven and enjoy!

7. Fan Favorite Bacon Mac & Cheese

<u>Ingredients</u>

1 Cup of Elbow Macaroni

¼ lb. of Bacon

2 Cups of Shredded Sharp Cheddar Cheese

½ Cup of Shredded Parmesan Cheese

2 Cup of Skim Milk

2 Tbs. of Butter + 1 Tbs.

½ Cup of Bread Crumbs

¾ Tbs. of Flour

1 Tbs. of Parsley

<u>Directions</u>:

1. Forget box macaroni and cheese! This homemade recipe is guaranteed to make your mouth water with its savory, cheesy bacon goodness. Start by cooking your macaroni according to the instructions provided on the packaging. And while your pasta is boiling, cook your bacon in the meantime.

2. Drain and rinse your pasta with cold water once it has finished cooking. Then, crumble your bacon strips into small bits to add in later.

3. Now is when the cheesy fun begins. Use the pot that you used for the macaroni to melt two tablespoons of butter. When the butter has melted, stir in the flour, followed by the milk. Allow the milk to heat up, but be sure to stir the ingredients frequently so that they do not burn onto the bottom of the pot.

4. Next, add the cheese into the pot, a little bit at a time until all the cheese has been melted.

5. Now, it is time to add in the macaroni and bacon! Stir in the noodles and bacon so that all of the ingredients combine.

6. Melt the rest of the butter into a separate pan, and then add in the bread crumbs and parsley leaves. Fry the contents of the pan until the bread crumbs turn golden brown.

7. Pour your macaroni into a serving bowl and spread the crumbs on top. Finally, place the dish into an oven at 350 degrees and bake for approximately forty minutes. Enjoy!

8. Sweet Potato Quesadilla

Ingredients

1 Sweet Potato

2 8- in. Whole- Wheat Tortilla

2 Tbs. of Feta Cheese, crumbled

5 Oz. of Sliced Chorizo

1 Tbs. of Coriander, roughly chopped

Directions:

1. Start by preheating your oven to 390 degrees and preparing a baking sheet with cooking spray and aluminum foil. Use a knife to pierce the sweet potatoes a few times, and then place the potatoes onto the tray.

2. Place the baking sheet in the oven and cook the potatoes for approximately fifty minutes, until they soften. Then, remove the tray from the oven and allow the potatoes to cool slightly.

3. Next, use a spoon to scoop out the potato flesh from the skins, spooning the potato into a bowl. Add the coriander into the bowl, and mash the sweet potato with a fork.

4. Now, add the feta cheese into the bowl and gently fold into the sweet potatoes.

5. Heat a skillet over medium heat and use a spoon to add the sweet potatoes onto half of each tortilla. Top the sweet potato filling with the chorizo slices, and then fold the other side of the tortilla over the filling to make a quesadilla.

6. Place your quesadilla onto the skillet and allow to cook for three minutes on each side, until the tortilla becomes a crispy golden brown.

7. Slice your quesadillas in half and enjoy with a side of sour cream!

9. Protein Powerhouse Sandwich

<u>Ingredients</u>

1 8- Oz. Can of Tuna, drained

2 Tbs. of Light Mayonnaise

2 Tbs. of Seed and Nut Mix

2 Tbs. of Snow Peas

1 Grated Carrot

1 Slice of Tomato

1 Handful of Shredded Lettuce

2 Slices of Whole- Grain Bread

<u>Directions:</u>

1. All you need to do for this recipe is mix together all of the ingredients together, excluding the bread slices of course.

2. When the ingredients are well integrated, simply spread the mixture on top of one slice of bread. Then, top your sandwich off with the second slice of whole- grain bread and enjoy!

10. Skinny Pizza

<u>Ingredients</u>

8 Oz. of Red Pepper and Tomato Salsa

1 Garlic and Coriander Naan Bread

¼ tsp. of Fennel Seeds (optional)

3 Tbs. of Ricotta Cheese

5 Oz. of Tomato and Mozzarella Salad

4 Stuffed Olives

Directions:

1. Preheat your oven to 420 degrees and prepare a baking sheet with cooking spray or aluminum foil.

2. Begin assembling your pizza by spooning the tomato and pepper salsa onto the naan bread, spreading the sauce to create an even layer on the top.

3. Next, lightly sprinkle the fennels seeds over the layer of sauce. Then, top with generous spoonfuls of ricotta cheese and the mozzarella- tomato salad.

4. Top your pizza with the stuffed olives and then place your lunch onto the baking sheet. Place the sheet into the oven and cook for approximately ten to twelve minutes, until the top layer of mozzarella has fully melted.

5. Remove the tray from the oven and allow your pizza to cool for a few minutes before serving. Enjoy!

11. Cheese and Hot Dog Bake

Ingredients

2 Eggs, beaten

4 Hot Dogs, cut into 1/4 – in. pieces

½ Cup of Pancake Mix

2 Tbs. of Yellow Onion, chopped

1 Cup of Shredded Cheddar Cheese

1 Cup of Milk

Directions:

1. Start by preheating your oven to 400 degrees and preparing a 9- in. pie plate with cooking spray. You can use a smaller pie dish if you are cutting the serving size down into a single serving.

2. Layer the hot dog pieces and diced onions in the pie dish. Then, in a medium- size mixing bowl, stir together the milk, pancake mix, and eggs with a whisk until the dough is blended together.

3. Pour the pancake powder and egg mixture into the pie dish, and sprinkle the cheddar cheese over top. Transfer the dish into the oven and bake for twenty-five minutes, until you can insert a knife into the center of the dish and have it come out clean.

4. Remove the hot dog bake from the oven and allow to cool for five minutes before enjoying with a side of ketchup and mustard.

12. Simple 3- Ingredient Mac & Cheese

Ingredients

1 Cup of Full Cream Milk

½ Cup of Elbow Macaroni

½ Cup of Shredded Cheddar Cheese

Directions:

1. This easy mac and cheese recipe is perfect if you are in a rush against the clock or are feeling too lazy to prepare an entire lunch. Start by pour the milk into a small saucepan and bring it to a boil over medium heat.

2. When the milk is bubbling, pour the pasta into the saucepan and bring the liquid to a boil once more.

3. Once the milk is boiling, reduce the heat and let simmer for approximately eight minutes. As the mixture thickens, stir in the cheese until the cheese melts into the pasta. Then, let the mac and cheese sit for two minutes before serving. Enjoy!

13. Vegetable Crumpets

Ingredients

½ Cup of Self-Rising Flour

1 Egg +1 Tbs. of a Beaten Egg

1 Cup of Mixed Vegetables, finely chopped

½ Tbs. of Milk + more, if necessary

¼ Cup of Shredded Cheddar Cheese

1 Tbs. of Extra Virgin Olive Oil

Directions:

1. Mix together the flour, vegetables, cheese, and eggs in a medium- size mixing bowl. Then, add in

enough milk to the mixture so that it becomes *slightly* runny.

2. Heat a skillet over medium heat and pour the olive oil into the pan. Spoon a tablespoon of the dough-mixture onto the frying pan and shape/ pat into an even circle. Repeat this process as many times as you need to, until all of the dough is used.

3. Cook the pikelets until they are golden brown on each side, turning each one over so that both sides cook evenly.

4. Transfer your pikelets onto a plate and enjoy with a serving of sour cream!

14. Mini Pineapple Pizza

<u>Ingredients</u>

2 English Muffins, sliced in half

3 Tbs. of Marinara Sauce, separated

2 Slices of Ham, diced

4 Oz. of Crushed Pineapple

1 Cup of Shredded Mozzarella Cheese

<u>Directions:</u>

1. Prepare to toast your English muffin pizzas by assembling your lunch accordingly. First, spread one and-a-half tablespoons of pizza sauce onto each of the muffin halves.

2. Next, generously place the ham and pineapple onto each muffin half on top of the marinara sauce. Finally, top off your pizzas with a heaping layer of mozzarella cheese.

3. Place the English muffin pizzas into the toaster oven, and cook to your preferred crispiness, or until the cheese is fully melted. Enjoy!

15. Spicy Buffalo Chicken Salad

Ingredients

1 Boneless, Skinless Chicken Breast

1 Tbs. of Unsalted Butter

1 Tbs. of Extra Virgin Olive Oil

½ Cup of Cayenne Pepper Hot Sauce

3 Cups of Mixed Leafy Greens

2 Tbs. of Blue Cheese Dressing

3 Tbs. of Crumbled Blue Cheese

Directions:

1. Use a knife to carefully slice the chicken breast in half lengthwise. Although this may be a bit tricky, the end result will be two evenly sized, thin chicken breasts.

2. Now, heat the butter and oil in a frying pan set over medium- high heat. Then, place the chicken breasts onto the skillet and cook on both sides until they are cooked through all the way; until each side is golden brown.

3. Once the chicken is finished cooking, remove from heat and pour off any excess oil or fat from the pan.

4. Next, place the chicken back into the frying pan and pour the hot sauce over top of the meat. Flip your chicken over, so that the sauce evenly coats both sides of the meat. Allow the breasts to sit in the hot sauce while you ready the remaining ingredients.

5. In a large bowl, toss together the mixed leafy greens with the blue cheese dressing. Then, sprinkle the blue cheese crumbles on top. Slice the chicken breasts into thin pieces and add them into the salad. Enjoy!

Chapter 4:
15 Quick Snack Recipes: Food in 10 Minutes or Less

1. Grilled Cheese Bites

<u>Ingredients</u>

4 Slices of American or Cheddar Cheese

1 Can of Crescent Rolls

3 Tbs. of Butter

<u>Directions:</u>

1. This recipe is super easy, and you can get as creative as you want by trying out different cheeses and other fun fillings. Start by unwrapping the cheese slices and popping open the can of crescent rolls.

2. Unroll each crescent and then fold each of the crescent rolls in half, and then into quarters. Fold the rolls in half once again.

3. Now, place half a slice of cheese into the center of each ball of dough. Then, roll the dough into a ball, so that the cheese is in the middle.

4. Preheat your oven according to the package instructions on the crescent roll tube, and prepare a baking sheet with aluminum foil or cooking spray. As the oven is heating up, melt the butter in a small dish.

5. Brush the melted butter onto each of the balls for added flavor and crispiness. Once your cheese balls

are all buttered up, place them onto the baking sheet. Transfer the baking sheet into the oven and bake according to the instructions provided on the crescents' packaging: approximately thirteen minutes.

6. Remove the baking sheet from the oven and enjoy the cheesy goodness!

2. Simple Spicy Popcorn

Ingredients

      1 ½ Tbs. of Canola Oil

      ¼ Cup of Popcorn Kernels

      1 ½ Tbs. of Butter

1 Tbs. of Sriracha

¾ tsp. of Salt

Directions:

1. This classic popcorn recipe makes for a great afterschool or movie time snack. First, coat the bottom of a medium- size pot with the canola oil. Then, pour the popcorn kernels into the pot and cover.

2. Place the pot over medium- high heat over the stove. When you heat the first few corn kernels begin to pop, start shaking the pot. Continue shaking the pot until all of the kernels have popped.

3. When the popping has completely stopped, remove the pot from heat and pour the popcorn into a large bowl.

4. While you are waiting for the popcorn to pop, just melt the butter in a small bowl using a microwave. Then, add the sriracha into the butter and stir together.

5. Drizzle the buttery seasoning over your popcorn and toss the contents of the bowl, so that all of the popcorn is covered with the sriracha. Enjoy!

3. Cool Mint and Pineapple Ice

Ingredients

20 Oz. of Pineapple Junks in juice, chilled in the refrigerator

2 Tbs. of Fresh Mint, chopped

Directions:

1. This recipe may take a few hours to fully freeze, but the preparation is super easy and the end result is definitely worth the wait; especially if you have a sweet tooth! Pour the contents of the pineapple can into an 8- in. square pan.

2. Cover the pan and place into the freezer for approximately two hours, until the pineapple and juice are almost frozen.

3. Once the pineapple is almost frozen, remove the pan from the freezer, and transfer into a food processor. Add the chopped mint leaves into the processor and pulse until smooth. Make sure not to

blend the ingredients too much, or else the pineapple juice will melt.

4. Serve your homemade pineapple ice immediately. Enjoy!

4. Low- Calorie Fruit Dip

<u>Ingredients</u>

>1 Cup of Low- Fat Sour Cream

>2 Tbs. of Light Brown Sugar

>2 Tbs. of Lime Juice

>1 tsp. pf Cinnamon Sugar

<u>Directions:</u>

1. This dip recipe is perfect for anyone who loves to eat fruit and can be eaten with any delicious ripened fruit. All you need to do is mix all of the ingredients together until the ingredients are completely incorporated, and then serve with your favorite fruit!

5. Classic Cheese Chex Mix

<u>Ingredients</u>

2 Cups of Chex Cereal

½ Cup of Cheese Crackers

½ tsp. of Garlic Powder

1 Cup of Mini Pretzels

6 Tbsp. of Grated Parmesan Cheese

¼ Stick of Butter, melted

Directions:

1. Simply add all of the ingredients together into a large bowl, and toss them together so that they are evenly blended.

2. Preheat your oven to 325 degrees and prepare a baking sheet with a light coating of cooking spray or parchment paper.

3. Once the oven is heated up, pour the Chex mix onto the baking sheet and evenly spread. Place the sheet into the oven for fifteen minutes, stirring occasionally so that the cereal does not burn.

4. Remove the tray from the oven and carefully pour your cheesy Chex mix back into the large bowl and enjoy!

6. Ham and Cheese Pinwheels

<u>Ingredients</u>

¼ Cup of Scallion Cream Cheese

1 Sun-Dried- Tomato Tortilla

2 Thin Slices of Ham

<u>Directions:</u>

1. Simply spread the cream cheese onto the tortilla. Then, place a layer of ham on top of the cheese.
2. Roll the tortilla up, and then carefully slice the roll into ½ -in. pieces.

7. Crunchy Chickpeas To Go

<u>Ingredients</u>

15 Oz. Can of Chickpeas

1 tsp. of Smoked Paprika

2 Tbs. of Extra Virgin Olive Oil

1 tsp. of Cumin

Directions:

1. Preheat your oven to 425 degrees. Drain the can of chickpeas, and then pour them into an ovenproof frying pan.

2. Next, add the olive oil into the skillet, along with the seasoning. You can even add a pinch of salt if you want a little extra flavor.

3. Pace the skillet into the oven and bake for twenty minutes. All you have to do once the chickpeas are done baking is pour them into a bowl and enjoy!

8. Sweet Cookie Dough Yogurt

Ingredients

6 Oz. of Low- Fat Greek Yogurt

2 tsp. of Chocolate Chips

1 Tbs. of Peanut Butter

1 Tbs. of Organic Honey

½ tsp. of Vanilla Extract

Directions:

1. Simple whisk all of the ingredients together in a small bowl until you achieve a smooth consistency.

2. Refrigerate the yogurt until you are ready to eat it. Enjoy!

9. Low- Cal Mozzarella Sticks

<u>Ingredients</u>

5 Egg Rolls Wrappers

5 Mozzarella Cheese Sticks

1 Large Egg

3 Tbs. of Extra Virgin Olive Oil

4 Tbs. of Marinara Sauce

<u>Directions:</u>

1. Unwrap each of the egg roll wrappers, and then place one mozzarella cheese stick onto the corner of each egg roll wrapper. Then, roll the mozzarella stick from the bottom.

2. Fold the corners of the wrapper into the stick as you continue rolling the cheese.

3. Crack the egg into a small bowl, and then whisk with a fork and add half a teaspoon of water into the

mixture. Now, lightly coat each wrapped cheese stick with the egg.

4. Heat a frying pan with the oil on medium- high heat. Fry the cheese sticks in the oil, turning so that all sides of the stick turn golden brown.

5. Remove the mozzarella sticks from the pan and serve them with sweet marinara sauce.

10. Sweet Potato Chips

Ingredients

2 Sweet Potatoes

Canola Oil Cooking Spray

½ Tbs. of Sea Salt

Directions:

1. First, wash the sweet potatoes and peel the skins off. Then, carefully slice the potatoes into equal-size thin circles, just like a regular potato chip.

2. Next, place a sheet of parchment paper onto the removable turntable that is inside your microwave. Lay the sweet potato slices onto the paper and lightly spray them with a coating of the canola oil cooking spray.

3. Sprinkle on the sea salt, and then place the turntable back into the microwave. Heat the potato slices in the microwave for four minutes.

4. Allow the chips to cool for a few seconds before serving. Enjoy!

11. Sweet Apple Stacks

<u>Ingredients</u>

2 Large Apples

¼ Cup of Peanut Butter

¼ Cup of Vanilla- Flavored Granola

2 Tbs. of Mini Chocolate Chips

<u>Directions:</u>

1. Start by slicing each apple into round rings. Try to slice at least four rings, so that you have enough to make multiple layers when you assemble your stacks.

2. Place one apple slice onto a plate, and spread a thin layer of peanut butter onto the fruit. Now, sprinkle a few chocolate chips and the granola onto the peanut butter.

3. Place another apple slice on top of the granola layer. You can either repeat this process once more, or

move onto the next apple sandwich. Continue assembling multiple apple stacks until you have used up all of the ingredients. Enjoy!

12. Frozen Yogurt Blueberries

Ingredients

16 Oz. of Fresh Blueberries

6 Oz. of Low- Fat Blueberry Greek Yogurt

Directions:

1. Before you begin preparing your blueberries, you must first wash them. Also, line a baking sheet with parchment paper.

2. Use a toothpick to dip each blueberry into the yogurt, so that the berry is fully coated with a full layer of yogurt. Place each berry onto the baking sheet. Repeat this process until you have used up all of the blueberries.

3. Next, simple put the baking sheet into the freezer and chill for one hour. Remove the baking sheet from the freezer and either enjoy your fruit right away, or store in the freezer inside a Ziploc bag for later.

13. Granola Energy Bites

<u>Ingredients</u>

1 Cup of Plan Oatmeal, *dry*

1/3 Cup of Honey

2/3 Cup of Toasted Coconut Flakes

1 tsp. of Vanilla Extract

½ Cup of Peanut Butter

¼ Cup of Ground Flaxseed

½ Cup of Dark Chocolate Chips

<u>Directions:</u>

1. Although this sweet snack will give you lots of energy, this recipe requires very little effort. Simply stir all of the ingredients in a mixing bowl until it is fully mixed.

2. Now, cover the bowl and refrigerate for thirty minutes. Remove the bowl from the fridge, and use your hands to roll 1- in. balls with the granola.

3. You can either enjoy this snack right away, or refrigerate in an airtight container for up to six days. Enjoy!

14. Cheesy Carrot Balls

Ingredients

½ Bar of Cold Cream Cheese

1 Carrot, finely grated

1 Cup of Cheddar Cheese, finely grated

Directions:

1. Use a wooden spoon to combine all of the ingredients together in a medium- size mixing bowl.

2. Then, use your hands to form 1- in. balls of the carrot- cheese mixture.

3. Either enjoy this snack right away, or refrigerate for up to two days with a plastic wrap covering.

15. Sweet Cinnamon Nachos

Ingredients

2 10-in. Whole- Wheat Tortillas

¼ tsp. of Cinnamon

1 Tbs. of Brown Sugar

1 ½ tsp. of Butter, at room temperature

Directions:

1. Heat your broiler, with the wire rack placed approximately four inches away from heat.

2. Place the tortillas onto a baking sheet lined with either parchment paper or aluminum foil.

3. In a small bowl, stir together the ground cinnamon and sugar. Then, divide the butter evenly and spread it onto each side of the tortillas.

4. Sprinkle the cinnamon- sugar mixture on top. Next, transfer the baking sheet into the oven and broil the tortillas until the sugar is golden brown. This should take approximately two minutes.

5. Remove the baking sheet from the oven and slice each tortilla into small wedges. Enjoy!

Chapter 5:
20 Dinner Recipes That Are Better Than Ordering Take- Out

1. Classic Sloppy Joes

<u>Ingredients</u>

> 1 Large Egg
>
> 1 Pound of Ground Beef
>
> 1 Onion, chopped
>
> 15 Oz. of Sloppy Joe Sauce
>
> 1 Cup of Shredded Cheddar Cheese
>
> 1 cup of Pancake Mix
>
> ½ Cup of Milk

<u>Directions:</u>

1. Preheat your oven to 400 degrees. Then, cook your ground beef in a large ovenproof frying pan for approximately ten minutes. Cook and stir the meat until it is no longer pink. Drain the excess grease from the pan, and then stir in the sauce.

2. Next, add the cheese into the pan and stir with the meat until it is fully melted into the mixture.

3. Combine the remaining ingredients in a separate bowl. Then, carefully pour the pancake powder mixture into the beef.

4. Place the skillet into the oven and cook, uncovered, for thirty minutes or until the crust is a light golden brown. Then, remove the skillet from the oven and enjoy!

2. Chicken Parmesan Sub- Sandwich

Ingredients

¼ Cup of Flour

1/3 Cup of Marinara Sauce

2 Boneless, Skinless Chicken Breasts

2 Tbs. of Parmesan Cheese

3 tsp. of Extra Virgin Olive Oil, separated

¼ Cup of Shredded Low- Fat Mozzarella Cheese

6 Oz. of Baby Spinach Leaves

2 Whole- Grain Sandwich Rolls, lightly toasted

Directions:

1. This recipe makes two servings, so it is perfect if you want to share with a sibling. Or, you can even double the ingredient measurements and prepare dinner for the whole family! Start by combining the flour with a dash of salt and pepper in a small, shallow dish.

2. Next, place the two chicken breasts between two pieces of plastic cling warp. Use a meat mallet or heavy frying pan to make the breasts thinner, so that they become ¼ -in. thick.

3. Now, coat the chicken breasts with the flour on either side.

4. Heat up one teaspoon of the olive oil a skillet. Place the flour- covered chicken into the frying pan and cook until the breast is golden brown on either side.

5. Now that you have turned over the chicken, so that it evenly cooks, you need to place a layer of spinach on top of the meat. Follow this layer with a spoonful of marinara sauce and parmesan cheese.

6. Finally, sprinkle the mozzarella cheese onto the chicken breasts and cover the frying pan. Allow the cheese to fully melt onto the meat, and then remove the breasts from the pan, onto the whole- grain rolls. Enjoy!

3. Zucchini Flatbread with Mixed Veggies

Ingredients

1 Small Zucchini, sliced into ½ -in. thick rounds

1 Tbs. of Chickpea Hummus

½ Tbs. of Extra Virgin Olive Oil

1 Tbs. of Chopped Almonds

2 Tbs. of Crumbled Goat Cheese

1 Round, Whole- Grain Pita, without the pocket

½ Cup of Baby Arugula

Directions:

1. Preheat your oven to 400 degrees and prepare a baking sheet with aluminum foil or parchment paper. Now, place the zucchini onto the sheet and drizzle the olive oil on top.

2. Place the baking sheet into the oven, and roast the zucchini until it is browned and tender. This should take approximately thirty minutes, and you must stir the vegetables halfway through the allotted time.

3. While the zucchini is cooking, warm the pita on the grill or in the toaster until the bread is lightly toasted, but still soft. Next, spread the hummus onto the pita, followed by a sprinkled layer of goat cheese.

4. Now, arrange the cooked zucchini onto the pita, and top with the arugula and almonds. Enjoy!

4. Chicken and Rice Soup

Ingredients

1/2 of a Chicken Breast, with the bone still in

1 Carrot, sliced into 2- in. pieces

½ Bay Leaf

3 Cups of Low- Sodium Chicken Stock

1 Tbs. of Butter

½ Onion, sliced very thin

½ tsp. of Sugar

¾ tsp. of Curry Powder

3 Tbs. of Jasmine Rice

1 Tbs. of Fresh Mint, chopped

1 Tbs. of Fresh Dill, chopped

½ of a Lemon

Directions:

1. In a medium- size saucepan, combine the carrots, chicken, and bay leaf. Then, stir in half of the chicken broth and bring the mixture to a boil over medium- high heat.

2. Once the soup is coming to a boil, reduce the heat to low setting and cover the saucepan. Allow the chicken to continue cooking for another fifteen minutes, until it is just starting to become firm.

3. While the chicken is cooking, melt the butter in a separate saucepan over medium- low heat. Place the chopped onion and sugar into the pan with a pinch of salt. Cook the mixture until the onion has softened.

4. Now, add the curry powder into the onion mixture and let cook for one minute. Add the rice and the rest of the chicken broth into the mixture and increase the heat of the saucepan to medium.

5. Cover the rice and let the ingredients simmer until the rice breaks apart. This will take approximately fifteen minutes.

6. Next, remove the chicken from the broth and remove the skin. Shred the breast into pieces with a fork, and then return it back into its sauce pan.

7. Pour the rice mixture into a blender and puree until you achieve a smooth consistency. Pour the rice mixture back into the sauce pan.

8. Now, pour the chicken and broth into the saucepan containing the rice, and carefully stir the ingredients together to combine the soup. Bring the soup to a simmer, and then serve with a dash of lemon juice.

5. Easy Chicken Meatballs

<u>Ingredients</u>

¼ of a Celery Stick, diced

2 Chives, snipped

½ of a Carrot, diced

1 lb. of Boneless, Skinless Chicken Thighs, sliced into chunks

1 Tbs. of Extra Virgin Olive Oil

<u>Directions:</u>

1. Preheat your oven to 400 degrees and prepare a baking sheet with aluminum foil and cooking spray.

2. Pulse the chicken, celery, chives, and carrot in a food processor until the mixture is finely chopped.

3. Use a spatula to scoop out the blended meat and transfer it into a bowl. Then, use your hands to shape the meat into small meatballs.

4. Place the meatballs onto the baking sheet, and the cook in the oven for approximately ten minutes, or until the meatballs are cooked through all the way.

5. Serve with a side of spaghetti or mixed vegetables.

6. **Potato and Cheddar Soup**

Ingredients

      1 Potato, peeled and chopped

      1 Vegetable Stock Cube

      1 zucchini, chopped

      2 Spring Onion, sliced

      3 Oz. of Grated Extra- Mature Cheddar Cheese

Directions:

1. Place the potato chunks into a medium pot, and add in just enough water to cover them. Then, crumble the vegetable stock cube into the water and bring the contents of the pot to a boil.

2. Allow the potato to cook for five minutes and before adding the spring onion to the pot. Cook for an addition five minutes.

3. Remove the pot from heat and stir the cheese into the potato mixture. Season your soup with salt, pepper, and nutmeg. Allow the liquid to cool slightly before enjoying with a side of whole- wheat crackers.

7. Homemade Chicken Pot Pie

<u>Ingredients</u>

¼ lb. of Parsnip, peeled

2 Tbs. of Low- Fat Crème Fraiche

2 Floury Potatoes, peeled

2 Leek, sliced

1 lb. of Boneless, Skinless Chicken Breasts

1 Tbs. of Corn flour

½ Tsp. of Extra Virgin Olive Oil

½ Tbs. of Mustard

<u>Directions:</u>

1. Preheat your oven to four hundred degrees and prepare a small, deep baking dish with cooking spray. Now, start by chopping the parsnips and potatoes into chunks, then boiling them together for approximately fifteen minutes over high heat.

2. Remove the potatoes from heat and drain the excess water into a bowl or later. Use a fork, hand mixer, or masher to mash the potatoes.

3. Next, slices the chicken breast in the small chunks, and then toss the meat in a bowl of corn flour to evenly coat each piece. Heat the olive oil in a frying pan over medium- high heat, and then place the chicken into the skillet.

4. Add the leeks into the frying pan and cook until the leaves are softened. Then, pour the excess water from the boiled potatoes into the skillet and bring the mixture to a boil.

5. Reduce the heat of the sauce pan and allow the contents to simmer for ten minutes. Then, add in the remaining ingredients and stir together into the baking dish.

6. Spoon the mashed potatoes over the top of the dish, and place in the oven. Bake the pie in the oven for twenty minutes, and enjoy!

8. Black Bean Chili for Two

<u>Ingredients</u>

> 2 Tbs. of Extra Virgin Olive Oil
>
> 1 Tbs. of Chili Powder
>
> 15 Oz. Can of Black Beans, rinsed
>
> 1 Onion, finely diced
>
> 1 Cup of Canned Diced Tomatoes
>
> 2 tsp. of Cumin
>
> 1 Sweet Potato, peeled and diced
>
> 1 Clove of Garlic, minced
>
> 1 1/3 Cups of Water

<u>Directions:</u>

1. Heat up the olive oil in a large saucepan over medium-high heat. Then, place the onion and potato into the pan and cook for approximately four minutes. Stir the vegetables often.

2. Next, add the spices and garlic into the saucepan and allow the flavors to cook into the vegetables for about half a minute. Then, add the water into the saucepan and bring the mixture to a simmer.

3. Cover the saucepan and reduce the heat so that the contents of the pan are lightly simmering. Cook for another ten minutes before adding the beans and tomatoes.

4. Increase the heat to a higher setting, returning the contents to a simmer. Be sure to stir the saucepan often to avoid the chili sticking to the bottom of the pan.

5. Reduce the heat of the saucepan and let simmer for another four minutes. Enjoy with a side of sour cream!

9. Greek Salad

Ingredients

2 ¼ Tbs. of Red Wine Vinegar

½ Tbs. of Extra Virgin Olive Oil

1 ½ Cups of Romaine Lettuce, chopped

½ tsp. of Oregano

¾ Cup of Cooked Chicken, chopped

¼ tsp. of Garlic Powder

2 Tbs. of Red Onion, finely chopped

1 Tomato, chopped

2 Tbs. of Black Olives

2 Tbs. of Feta Cheese, crumbled

A Dash of Salt

A Dash of Pepper

Directions:

1. Start making your salad dressing by whisking together the vinegar, oregano, garlic powder, olive oil, salt, and pepper in a bowl until evenly combined.

2. Now, add the remaining ingredients into the bowl, and toss your salad so that the dressing evenly coats the lettuce and chicken. Enjoy!

10.   Shrimp and Garlic Pasta for Two

Ingredients

3 Oz. of Whole- Wheat Spaghetti

¾ Cup of Low- Fat Yogurt

½ Cup of Peas, fresh or frozen

2 Tbs. of Fresh Parsley, chopped

6 Oz. of Raw Shrimp, peeled, deveined, and sliced into 1- in. pieces

½ of a Red Bell Pepper, sliced thin

1 Tbs. of Lemon Juice

1 Garlic Clove, chopped

½ Bunch of Asparagus, trimmed and sliced thing

1 ½ tsp. of Extra Virgin Olive Oil

Salt and Pepper to Taste

Directions:

1. Start by bringing a large pot of water to a boil, and then add in the pasta. Cook the spaghetti for two minutes less than what the packaging suggests.

2. While the spaghetti is about to finish cooking, add the shrimp, pepper, peas, and asparagus to the pot. Continue cooking the ingredients until the pasta is tender and the shrimp are cooked through.

3. Next, drain the pasta of excess water. In a large bowl, mash the garlic and salt until it has the consistency of a paste. Now, whisk the yogurt, lemon, parsley, oil, and pepper into the sauce.

4. Pour the pasta- shrimp mixture into the sauce, and toss so that the ingredients are fully coated with the garlic sauce. Enjoy!

11. Hearty Beef Stew

Ingredients

2 ½ tsp. of Canola Oil, separated

2 tsp. of Flour

8 Oz. of Bottom-Round Beef Cubes

1 Cup of Low- Sodium Beef Broth

1 Large Shallot, thinly sliced

2 Cups of Butternut Squash, peeled and cubed

1 tsp. of Thyme

½ tsp. of Rubbed Sage

1/3 Cup of Dried Cherries

Salt and Pepper to Taste

Directions:

1. Preheat your oven to 350 degrees. Then, bring 1 ½ teaspoons of the canola oil to heat over medium-heat in a large saucepan. Place the beef cubes into the saucepan and cook the meat until it is browned on all sides.

2. Remove the meat from the stove and transfer onto a separate plate. Turn your oven to medium- low setting, and add the last teaspoon of the oil into the pan with the shallot. Cook the shallot for one minute, continuously stirring.

3. Now, add in the sage, salt, pepper, and thyme into the pan. After a few seconds, transfer the beef cubes back into the pan and evenly sprinkle the flour on top.

4. Cook and stir the mixture until the flour browns; this should take approximately three minutest.

5. Then, pour the broth into the pan and cook for another two minutes, stirring continuously. Add in the squash, and then cover the pan.

6. Place the saucepan into the oven and cook for one hour. Then, add the cherries into the stew and continue cooking for another twenty- five minutes. Enjoy with a side of mashed potatoes and whole-grain bread!

12. Chicken Masala

<u>Ingredients</u>

> 1 tsp. of Garam Masala
>
> 4 Oz. of Chicken Tenders
>
> ½ Sweet Onion, diced
>
> 1/8 tsp. of Turmeric
>
> 1 tsp. of Fresh Ginger, minced
>
> 1 tsp. of Canola Oil
>
> 8 Oz. of Canned Diced Tomatoes, undrained
>
> 2 Tbs. of Flour
>
> 1 Tbs. of Whipping Cream
>
> 1 ½ Cloves of Garlic, minced
>
> Salt and Pepper to Taste

<u>Directions:</u>

1. Start by whisking together the garam masala, turmeric, and salt into a small bowl. Also, pour the flour onto a large plate or shallow dish.

2. Evenly sprinkle the chicken with one-fourth a teaspoon of the spice seasoning, and then cover with a thin layer of flour.

3. Over medium- high heat, warm half of the canola oil in a frying pan. Cook the chicken in the pan until it becomes golden brown. Then, transfer the chicken onto a plate for later.

4. Heat up the last of the canola oil in the frying pan and reduce heat to medium- low. Add the ginger, garlic, and onion into the pan and cook until the vegetables start to brown. Add in one teaspoon of the flour to the vegetables and stir the contents of the pan until they are evenly coated with the flour.

5. Pour in the rest of the spice seasoning into the skillet, along with the can of tomatoes. Now, bring the mixture to a simmer and allow the sauce to thicken. Cook until the onion is tender.

6. Next, stir the cream into the skillet before add in the chicken. Bring the chicken to a simmer and allow to cook for another four minutes. Enjoy with a side of mixed vegetables!

13. Tangy BBQ Ribs

Ingredients

1 Rack of Pork Spare Ribs

1/3 Small Onion, diced

1/3 Tbs. of Extra Virgin Olive Oil

½ Clove of Garlic, crushed

½ Tbs. of Paprika

½ tsp. of Chili Powder

1 Cup of Tomato Passata

½ Tbs. of Tomato Puree

1/3 Cup of Red or White Wine Vinegar

2 Oz. of Dark Muscovado Sugar

Directions:

1. Preheat your oven to 300 degrees and ready a roasting tin. Place the stack of ribs into the roasting tin and cover with water. Cover the tin with a layer of aluminum foil, and cook in the oven for one hour and thirty minutes.

2. When the ribs are finished cooking, drain out the water. While the ribs are cooking, heat the oil in a skillet and cook the onion until softened. Then, add in the passata, vinegar, tomato puree, and dark sugar. Mix the ingredients together and bring the mixture to a simmer. Let cook for ten minutes.

3. Brush the ribs with your homemade sauce, and then carefully slice the ribs, so that they are ready to serve.

14. Chicken Chow Mein

<u>Ingredients</u>

<u>For the Sauce:</u>

1-in. Size Piece of Ginger

2 Cloves of Garlic

3 Tbs. of Ketchup

2 Tbs. of Oyster Sauce

2 Tbs. of Low- Sodium Soy Sauce

<u>For the Chow Mein</u>

1 Red Bell Pepper, sliced into thin strips

1 Large Chicken Breast

4 Spring Onions

1 Tbs. of Sunflower Oil

3 Nests of Egg Noodles

8 Oz. of Beansprouts

<u>Directions:</u>

1. Peel the skin off of the ginger using a potato peeler. Then, carefully grate a tablespoon of ginger from the root into a bowl. Add the garlic into the bowl and crush the clove. Now, add in the soy sauce, ketchup, oyster sauce, and three tablespoons of water. Stir the mixture to combine all of the ingredients.

2. Now, it is time to work on the chicken chow mien. Start by cutting the end off of the spring onions and slicing the green and white of the onion lengthwise.

3. Cut the chicken into small cubes.

4. Next, bring a large pot of water to a boil and add the noodles into the pot. Turn off the stove and let the pasta cook for four minutes. Then, drain the pasta.

5. Heat a wok so that it starts to slightly smoke, then add in the oil and chicken. Using a wooden spoon, stir the chicken in the walk until to turns half white, half pink.

6. Add in the red pepper and continue cooking for another minute. Next, pour the sauce into the wok and stir until the sauce starts bubbling.

7. Finally, add in the remaining ingredients, one handful at a time. Toss the contents of the wok with the sauce until the noodles are evenly coated. Serve and enjoy!

15. Chicken and Carrot Pie

<u>Ingredients</u>

1 Small Carrot

1 tbs. of Melted Butter

1/2 Potato

½ Slice of Cooked Ham

2 Tbs. of Double Cream

1 Boneless, Skinless Chicken Breast

1 ½ Tbs. of Frozen Peas, defrosted

Directions:

1. Heat your oven to 390 degrees and prepare a small pie dish with cooking spray.

2. Bring a pot of water to a boil over high heat, and add in the carrot and potato. Boil the vegetables for five minutes. Then, carefully transfer the potato and carrot to a bowl of cold water.

3. Peel the potato and carrot with a potato peeler, and then grate them into a large bowl.

4. Next, add the melted butter into the bowl and mix the ingredients together.

5. Slice the ham into small bite- size pieces, as well as the chicken. Then, place the meat into the pie dish, topped with the peas and cream. Stir the contents of the pie dish together.

6. Spoon the potato and carrot mixture on top of the pie, and then place the dish in the oven. Cook for fifty minutes, until the chicken is cooked through. Then, carefully remove the dish from the oven and allow to cool for a few minutes before eating. Enjoy!

16. Lemon and Sesame Chicken

Ingredients

4 Boneless, Skinless Chicken Thighs

1 tsp. of Sesame Oil

1 tsp. of Sesame Seeds

1 tsp. of Corn Flour

Zest and Juice from 1 Lemon

1 Tbs. of Honey

1 Tbs. of Low- Sodium Soy Sauce

Directions:

1. Preheat your oven to 430 degrees. Place the chicken in a shallow roasting tin and coat with the sesame oil. Transfer the roasting tin into the oven and cook the chicken for twenty- five minutes.

2. While the chicken is cooking, begin making the sauce. Pour the corn flour into a medium bowl, and whisk it with the lemon juice and zest until the mixture is smooth. Add in the soy sauce, honey, and sesame seeds, and mix the sauce once again until smooth.

3. Remove the chicken from the oven, and carefully pour an even layer of sauce over the meat so that it is nicely coated. Place the chicken back into the oven and continue cooking for another ten minutes. Carefully spoon the sauce over the chicken every three minutes as it begins to thicken.

4. Serve your savory chicken with a side of noodles or vegetables. Enjoy!

17. Teriyaki Salmon

Ingredients

1 Tbs. of Soy Sauce

½ Clove of Garlic, finely chopped

½ Tbs. of Honey

2 tsp. of Sunflower Oil

½ Cup of Steamed Broccoli Florets

1 Salmon Fillet

Directions:

1. Preheat your oven to 390 degrees. Then, begin your recipe by making the teriyaki sauce. In a small bowl, whisk the honey, mirin, garlic, and soy sauce together so that the ingredients are well combined.

2. Use scissors to cut one square of aluminum foil, about thirty centimeters' square. Then, lightly brush a little bit of the oil onto the foil and slightly fold up the edges of the foil.

3. Next, place the broccoli into the foil and then reset the salmon fillet on top.

4. Spoon the sauce over the fillet and then fold the edges of the little foil parcel over the salmon to seal it inside the foil pocket.

5. Place the salmon pocket onto a baking sheet, and then transfer the sheet into the oven. Cook for approximately fifteen to eighteen minutes. When the salmon is finished cooking, remove the tray from the oven and carefully transfer the salmon and broccoli onto a plate. Enjoy with a side of rice!

18.Simple Roast Chicken

<u>Ingredients</u>

1 Whole Chicken, weighing around 2 pounds

1 Lemon, sliced in half

3 Carrots, cut into bite- size chunks

1 Tbs. of Low- Sodium Soy Sauce

3 Small Potatoes, cut into bite- size pieces

2 Cloves of Garlic

1 Tbs. of Extra Virgin Olive Oil

2 Oz. of Softened Butter

1 ¼ Cups of Chicken Stock

<u>Directions:</u>

1. Cooking an entire chicken may seem like a huge task for a teen in the kitchen, but it is much easier than you realize. As long as you follow the instructions and pay attention to the cooking time, you will have a delicious chicken dinner even if you are just learning how to cook!

2. Preheat your oven to 430 degrees. Use a pair of scissors to cut the off that string that is holding the chicken's legs together. Place the chicken into a roasting tin. Now, stuff the chicken with the lemon halves and garlic. Yes, you must put your hands inside the chicken to do this.

3. Now it is time to get even messier! Use your hands to smear the butter all over the chicken.

4. Now, pour the carrots and potatoes into a medium-size mixing bowl and drizzle the oil on top of the vegetable. Toss the veggie bowl using your hands, so that the oil evenly coats the vegetables

5. Place the vegetables around the chicken in an even layer. Then, season your dinner with salt and pepper.

6. Now, place the chicken into the oven and cook for thirty minutes. After half an hour, remove the roasting tin from the oven and stir the vegetables.

7. Reduce the heat of the oven to 390 degrees and return the chicken back into the oven. Continue cooking the chicken for another fifty minutes.

8. Now, it is time to check if the chicken is cooked. Remove the chicken from the oven and pull the leg away from the body of the chicken. If there is no pink in the meat and the juices are running clear, then the chicken is all cooked!

9. Next, spoon out the vegetables from the roasting pin and into a serving dish. Then, insert a pair of tongs into the chicken and remove the garlic and lemon to discard.

10. Strain the sauce by pouring the chicken stock and soy sauce into the tin with the chicken. Remove the chicken from the roasting tin and stir the sauce together with the juices in the pan. Use a spoon to scoop the sauce over top of the chicken.

11. Carefully slice the chicken and serve!

19.Stuffed Mushrooms

<u>Ingredients</u>

2 Large Portobello Mushrooms, stems and gills removed

2 Tbs. of Grated Parmesan Cheese

½ Tbs. of Low- Fat Italian Salad Dressing

6 Oz. of Baby Spinach Leaves, chopped

1 ½ Tbs. of Seasoned Bread Crumbs, seperated

1 Egg

½ Clove of Garlic, minced

2 Tbs. of Shredded Mozzarella Cheese, separated

2 Tbs. of Chopped Pepperoni

Salt and Pepper to taste

<u>Directions:</u>

1. Preheat the oven to 350 degrees and prepare a baking sheet with cooking spray.

2. Brush both sides of the Portobello mushroom caps with the Italian dressing, and then place them onto the baking sheet with the gills facing up.

3. Place the mushrooms in the oven and bake for approximately twelve minutes, until the mushrooms become tender. After the time is up, drain any juices that leaked into the mushroom caps.

4. While the mushrooms are cooking, beat the egg, salt, pepper, and garlic in a bowl.

5. Now, add the pepperoni, parmesan, spinach, and half of the mozzarella cheese and breadcrumbs. Stir together so that the ingredients are evenly mixed.

6. Now, divide the spinach and egg mixture into the mushroom caps and sprinkle the rest of the cheese on top. Then, place the mushrooms back into the oven and continue baking for another ten minutes.

7. When the cheese is melted, remove the tray from the oven and allow to cool slightly before serving. Enjoy!

20.   Turkey and Broccoli Pasta Dish

Ingredients

¼ lb. of Orecchiette

1 Clove of Garlic, chopped

1 Cup of Broccoli Florets

½ tsp. of Fennel Seed

1 ½ Tbs. of Extra Virgin Olive Oil

½ lb. of Ground Turkey

¼ tsp. of Crushed Red Pepper

Directions:

1. Cook the pasta in accordance with the instructions provided on the packaging.

2. About two minutes before the pasta is finished cooking, add the broccoli florets into the pot. When the pasta is done, drain and then add the noodles and broccoli back into the pot.

3. While the pasta is cooking, heat half of the olive oil in a large skillet over medium- high heat. Next, add the ground turkey, red pepper, and fennel seeds into the skillet and cook until the meat is browned. This should take approximately four to five minutes.

4. Now, toss the turkey and remaining olive into the pot with the pasta and broccoli. Serve and enjoy!

Chapter 6:
10 Sweet, But Healthy Desserts

1. Low- Cal Milkshake Pops

<u>Ingredients</u>

405ml of Light Condensed Milk

8 Strawberries

1 Banana, chopped

1 tsp. of Vanilla Bean Paste

<u>Directions:</u>

1. Simply add all of the ingredients into a food processor and pulse until you achieve a smooth consistency.

2. Now, divide the mixture into for paper cups, then cover the cups with aluminum foil. Then, push a popsicle stick into each foil lid until it reached the bottom of the cup.

3. Put the cups into the freezer and freeze for four hours. Enjoy!

2. Sweet Coconut Macaroons

<u>Ingredients</u>

2 ¾ Cup of Shredded Coconut

7 Oz. Can of Sweetened Condensed Milk

1 tsp. of Vanilla Extract

Directions:

1. Preheat your oven to 325 degrees and prepare a baking sheet with parchment paper.

2. In a large bowl, combine all of the ingredients together so that the mixture is blended well.

3. Use a teaspoon to scoop the batter onto the baking sheet. Place the baking sheet into the oven and bake for approximately ten minutes; until the edges are lightly browned.

4. Remove the baking sheet from the oven and allow the cookies to cool before serving.

3. Peanut Butter Ice Cream

Ingredients

4 Large Bananas, extra ripened

2 Tbs. of Smooth Peanut Butter

Directions:

1. Peel the bananas and slice them into the ½ -in. pieces. Then place the banana slices onto a baking sheet lined with parchment paper. Place the baking sheet in the freezer for one hour and thirty minutes.

2. Remove the banana slices and add them into a food processor. Puree the slices until you achieve a smooth and creamy texture.

3. Add in the peanut butter, and combine with the frozen banana puree.

4. Serve the ice cream immediately and enjoy!

4. Cherries and Ricotta

Ingredients

> ¾ Cup of Frozen, Pitted Cherries
>
> 1 Tbs. of Toasted, Toasted Almonds
>
> 2 Tbs. of Part- Skim Ricotta

Directions:

1. First, heat the cherries in the microwave for one minute and thirty seconds.

2. Scoop the ricotta cheese into a small bowl, and mix in the cherries and almonds. Enjoy!

5. Banana Chocolate Chip Cookies

Ingredients

> 1 Cup of Oat Flour
>
> ¾ Cup of Rolled Oats
>
> 1/3 Cup of Dark Chocolate Chips
>
> ½ tsp. of Baking Powder
>
> ¼ Cup of Chopped Walnuts
>
> 1/3 tsp. of Baking Soda

½ Ripe Banana, sliced into ½- in. pieces

½ tsp. of Salt

½ Cup of Sugar

½ tsp. of Vanilla Extract

1/3 Cup of Canola Oil

1/3 Cup of Soy Milk

Directions:

1. Preheat your oven to 350 degrees and prepare a baking sheet with parchment paper. In a medium bowl, combine the oat flour, rolled oats, baking powder, baking soda, salt, and sugar.

2. In a separate bowl, whisk the milk, vanilla, and oil. Now, add the wet mixture into the dry mixture of ingredients. Stir the ingredients together until well combined.

3. Next, fold the banana, chocolate, and walnuts into the cookie dough. Use a tablespoon to scoop the dough onto the baking sheet. Place the sheet into the oven and cook for twenty- five minutes; until the cookies turn golden brown.

4. Remove the baking sheet from the oven and allow the cookies to cool on a wire rack. Enjoy!

6. Sweet Baked Pears

Ingredients

1 Large Bosc Pear

1 tsp. of Sugar

1/8 tsp. of Cinnamon

2 Tbs. of Dried Cranberries

2 Tbs. of Granola

2 Tbs. of Apple Juice

¼ Cup of Vanilla Frozen Yogurt

Directions:

1. First, carefully peel the pear and then slice the fruit in half lengthwise. Use a small spoon to remove the core and seeds from the pear halves to create a hollow in the fruit.

2. In a small bowl, combine the sugar and cinnamon. Place the pear halves onto a microwave safe dish, with the cut side facing up. Sprinkle the cinnamon sugar on top of the fruit.

3. In another bowl, stir together the cranberries and granola, then spoon the mixture into the hollows of the pears.

4. Now, carefully pour the apple juice inside the hallows and onto the fruit.

5. Loosely cover the baking dish with wax paper. Place the pears into the microwave for seven minutes; until the fruit is tender enough that you can pierce it with a knife.

6. Let the pears cool in the microwave for a few minutes before enjoying!

7. **Sweet Broiled Nectarines**

Ingredients

>2 Large Nectarines, halved and pitted
>
>2 Tbs. of Honey
>
>1 Tbs. of Lemon Juice

Directions:

1. Preheat your broiler and prepare a baking pan with parchment paper.

2. Place the nectarines onto the pan with the cut side facing up.

3. In a small bowl, mix together the honey and lemon juice. Then, brush the mixture on top of the nectarines.

4. Place the baking pan into the broiler for seven minutes, and serve warm!

8. **Raspberry Cream**

Ingredients

>½ Cup of Raspberry Jam
>
>1 ¼ Cup of Heavy Cream
>
>1 Tbs. of Sugar
>
>1 Cup of Raspberries
>
>2 Shortbread Cookies

Directions:

1. Pour the heavy cream into a large bowl with the sugar. Then, use a handheld mixer to beat the heavy cream until stiff peaks form.

2. In a separate bowl, whisk the jam until it becomes smooth. Then, fold the jam into the heavy cream mixture.

3. Serve this fruity dessert with a garnish of shortbread cookies and enjoy!

9. Easy Chocolate Mug Cake

Ingredients

¼ tsp. of Baking Powder

1/8 Cup of Creamy Peanut Butter

1 ½ Tbs. of Dark Chocolate Chips

1 Tbs. of Applesauce

1/8 tsp. of Vanilla Extract

2 Tbs. of Organic Honey

1 Tbs. Dark Chocolate Cocoa Powder

1 Egg

1 ½ Tbs. of Oat Flour

1/8 tsp. of Salt

½ tsp. of Coconut Flour

Directions:

1. Start by first melting the peanut butter into the microwave in a mug for thirty seconds.

2. Now, add the rest of the ingredients into the mug and stir so that you achieve a well- combined cake batter.

3. Place the mug into the microwave and heat for ninety seconds. Enjoy!

10. **Simple Peanut Butter Cookies**

Ingredients

1 Cup of Creamy Peanut Butter

1 Egg

1 Cup of Sugar

Directions:

1. Preheat your oven to 350 degrees and prepare a baking sheet with parchment paper or cooking spray.

2. In a large bowl, combine all of the ingredients until you achieve a smooth batter.

3. Use a spoon to scoop the dough onto the baking sheet and place the cookies into the oven. Bake for six to seven minutes, but be sure not to overbake the cookies, or else they will fall apart! Enjoy!

Conclusion

Thank you again for downloading this book!

I hope this book was able to help you to understand the basics of cooking and inspire you to try your hand at learning your way around the kitchen! Every skill comes with a lot of practice. The key is to keep trying new recipes and mastering them until your food comes out perfect every time.

Finally, if you enjoyed this book, please take the time to share your thoughts and post a review on Amazon. It'd be greatly appreciated!

Thank you and good luck!